CONVENTION BETWEEN THE

UNITED STATES OF AMERICA AND THE

REPUBLIC OF ESTONIA FOR THE AVOIDANCE OF

DOUBLE TAXATION AND THE PREVENTION OF FISCAL EVASION

WITH RESPECT TO TAXES ON INCOME

The United States of America and the Republic of Estonia, desiring to conclude a Convention for the avoidance of double taxation and the prevention of fiscal evasion with respect to taxes on income, have agreed as follows:

ARTICLE 1

General Scope

1. This Convention shall apply to persons who are residents of one or both of the Contracting States, except as otherwise provided in the Convention.

2. The Convention shall not restrict in any manner any exclusion, exemption, deduction, credit, or other allowance now or hereafter accorded:

    a) by the laws of either Contracting State; or

    b) by any other agreement between the Contracting States.

3. Notwithstanding the provisions of subparagraph 2 b):

    a) the provisions of Article 26 (Mutual Agreement Procedure) of this Convention exclusively shall apply to any dispute concerning whether a measure is within the scope of this Convention, and the procedures under this Convention exclusively shall apply to that dispute; and

    b) unless the competent authorities determine that a taxation measure is not within the scope of this Convention, the nondiscrimination obligations of this Convention exclusively shall apply with respect to that measure, except for such national treatment or most-favored-nation obligations as may apply to trade in goods under the General Agreement on Tariffs and Trade.

No national treatment or most-favored-nation obligation under any other agreement shall apply with respect to that measure.

c) For the purpose of this paragraph, a "measure" is a law, regulation, rule, procedure, decision, administrative action, or any similar provision or action.

4. Notwithstanding any provision of the Convention except paragraph 5 of this Article, a Contracting State may tax its residents (as determined under Article 4 (Resident)), and by reason of citizenship may tax its citizens, as if the Convention had not come into effect. For this purpose, the term "citizen" shall include a former citizen or long-term resident whose loss of such status had as one of its principal purposes the avoidance of tax, but only for a period of 10 years following such loss.

5. The provisions of paragraph 4 shall not affect:

a) the benefits conferred by a Contracting State under paragraph 2 of Article 9 (Associated Enterprises), under paragraphs 2 and 5 of Article 18 (Pensions, Social Security, Annuities, Alimony, and Child Support), and under Articles 23 (Relief from Double Taxation), 24 (Nondiscrimination), and 25 (Mutual Agreement Procedure); and

b) the benefits conferred by a Contracting State

under Articles 19 (Government Service), 20 (Students, Trainees and Researchers), and 27 (Members of Diplomatic Missions and Consular Posts), upon individuals who are neither citizens of, nor have been admitted for permanent residence in, that State.

ARTICLE 2

Taxes Covered

1. The existing taxes to which the Convention shall apply are:

a) in the United States: the Federal income taxes imposed by the Internal Revenue Code (but excluding the accumulated earnings tax, the personal holding company tax, and social security taxes), and the excise taxes imposed with respect to the investment income of private foundations (hereafter referred to as "United States tax");

b) in Estonia: the income tax (tulumaks) (but excluding the tax on insurance companies provided in paragraph 35 of the Estonian income tax law), and the local income tax (kohalik tulumaks), (hereafter referred to as "Estonian tax").

2. The Convention shall apply also to any identical or substantially similar taxes which are imposed after the date of signature of the Convention in addition to, or in

place of, the existing taxes. The competent authorities of the Contracting States shall notify each other of any significant changes which have been made in their respective taxation laws or other laws affecting their obligations under the Convention, and of any official published material concerning the application of the Convention, including explanations, regulations, rulings, or judicial decisions.

ARTICLE 3

General Definitions

1.   For the purposes of this Convention, unless the context otherwise requires:

a) the term "Contracting State" means the United States or Estonia as the context requires;

b) the term "United States" means the United States of America, but does not include Puerto Rico, the Virgin Islands, Guam, or any other United States possession or territory. When used in a geographical sense, the term "United States" includes any area adjacent to the territorial waters of the United States within which under the laws of the United States and in accordance with international law, the rights of the United States may be exercised with respect to the sea bed and its sub-soil and their natural resources;

c) the term "Estonia" means the Republic of

Estonia and, when used in a geographical sense means the territory of Estonia and any other area adjacent to the territorial waters of Estonia within which under the laws of Estonia and in accordance with international law, the rights of Estonia may be exercised with respect to the sea bed and its sub-soil and their natural resources;

d) the term "person" includes an individual, an estate, a trust, a partnership, a company, and any other body of persons;

e) the term "company" means any body corporate or any entity which is treated as a body corporate for tax purposes;

f) the terms "enterprise of a Contracting State" and "enterprise of the other Contracting State" mean, respectively, an enterprise carried on by a resident of a Contracting State and an enterprise carried on by a resident of the other Contracting State;

g) the term "international traffic" means any transport by a ship or aircraft operated by an enterprise of a Contracting State, except when such transport is solely between places in the other Contracting State;

h) the term "competent authority" means:

(i) in the United States, the Secretary of the Treasury or his delegate; and

(ii) in Estonia, the Minister of Finance or his authorized representative;

i) the term "national" means:

(i) any individual possessing the nationality of a Contracting State; and

(ii) any legal person, partnership or association deriving its status as such from the laws in force in a Contracting State.

2. As regards the application of the Convention at any time by a Contracting State, any term not defined herein shall, unless the context otherwise requires or the competent authorities agree to a common meaning pursuant to the provisions of Article 25 (Mutual Agreement Procedure), have the meaning which it has at that time under the laws of that State for the purposes of the taxes to which the Convention applies, any meaning under the applicable tax laws of that State prevailing over a meaning given to the

term under other laws of that State.

ARTICLE 4

Resident

1.   For the purposes of this Convention, the term "resident of a Contracting State" means any person who, under the laws of that State, is liable to tax therein by reason of his residence, domicile, citizenship, place of management, place of incorporation, or any other criterion of a similar nature.

2.   a) However, the term "resident of a Contracting State" does not include any person who is liable to tax in that State in respect only of income from sources in that State;

b) in the case of income derived or paid by a partnership, estate, or trust, this term applies only to the extent that the income derived by such partnership, estate, or trust is subject to tax in that State as the income of a resident, either in its hands or in the hands of its partners or beneficiaries; and

c) if an individual is liable to tax as a resident because the individual is a citizen or permanent resident of a Contracting State and such resident is not also a resident of the other Contracting State, then the other State shall consider that individual to be a resident of the first-mentioned State only if the individual has a substantial presence, permanent home or habitual abode in the first-mentioned State. If the individual is a resident of both Contracting States, his State of residence shall be determined under paragraph 4.

3.   The term "resident of a Contracting State" includes:

a) that State, a political subdivision, or a local authority thereof, and any agency or instrumentality of any such State, subdivision or authority; and

b) a legal person organized under the laws of a Contracting State and that is generally exempt from tax in that State because it is established and maintained in that State either:

(i) exclusively for a religious, charitable, educational, scientific, or other similar purpose; or

(ii) to provide pensions or other similar benefits to employees pursuant to a plan.

4.   Where by reason of the provisions of paragraph 1 an individual is a resident of both Contracting States, then his status shall be determined as follows:

a) he shall be deemed to be a resident of the State in which he has a permanent home available to him; if he has a permanent home available to him in both States, he shall be deemed to be a resident of the State with which his personal and economic relations are closer (center of vital interests);

b) if the State in which he has his center of vital interests cannot be determined, or if he does not have a permanent home available to him in either State, he shall be deemed to be a resident of the State in which he has an habitual abode;

c) if he has an habitual abode in both States or in neither of them, he shall be deemed to be a resident of the State of which he is a national;

d) if he is a national of both States or of neither of them, the competent authorities of the Contracting States shall settle the question by mutual agreement.

5.   Where by reason of the provisions of paragraph 1 a company is a resident of both Contracting States, the competent authorities of the Contracting States shall endeavor to settle the question by mutual agreement. In the

absence of such agreement, such company shall not be considered to be a resident of either Contracting State for the purposes of enjoying benefits under this Convention.

6.   Where by reason of the provisions of paragraph 1 a person other than an individual or a company is a resident of both Contracting States, the competent authorities of the Contracting States shall settle the question by mutual agreement and determine the mode of application of the Convention to such person.

ARTICLE 5

Permanent Establishment

1.   For the purposes of this Convention, the term "permanent establishment" means a fixed place of business through which the business of an enterprise is wholly or partly carried on.

2.   The term "permanent establishment" includes especially

    a) a place of management;

    b) a branch;

    c) an office;

    d) a factory;

    e) a workshop; and

    f) a mine, an oil or gas well, a quarry, or any other place of extraction of natural resources.

3.   The term "permanent establishment" also includes a building site or construction or installation project, or an installation or drilling rig or ship used for the exploration or exploitation of natural resources, but only if it lasts more than 6 months.

4.   Notwithstanding the preceding provisions of this Article, the term "permanent establishment" shall be deemed not to include:

a) the use of facilities solely for the purpose of storage, display, or delivery of goods or merchandise belonging to the enterprise;

b) the maintenance of a stock of goods or merchandise belonging to the enterprise solely for the purpose of storage, display, or delivery;

c) the maintenance of a stock of goods or merchandise belonging to the enterprise solely for the purpose of processing by another enterprise;

d) the maintenance of a fixed place of business solely for the purpose of purchasing goods or merchandise, or of collecting information, for the enterprise;

e) the maintenance of a fixed place of business solely for the purpose of carrying on, for the enterprise, any other activity of a preparatory or auxiliary character;

f) the maintenance of a fixed place of business solely for any combination of the activities mentioned in subparagraphs a) to e), provided that the overall activity of the fixed place of business resulting from this combination is of a preparatory or auxiliary character.

5. Notwithstanding the provisions of paragraphs 1 and 2, where a person (other than an agent of an independent status to whom paragraph 6 applies) is acting on behalf of an enterprise and has, and habitually exercises, in a Contracting State an authority to conclude contracts in the name of the enterprise, that enterprise shall be deemed to have a permanent establishment in that State in respect of any activities which that person undertakes for the enterprise, unless the activities of such person are limited to those mentioned in paragraph 4 which, if exercised through a fixed place of business, would not make this fixed place of business a permanent establishment under the provisions of that paragraph.

6.   An enterprise shall not be deemed to have a permanent establishment in a Contracting State merely because it carries on business in that State through a broker, general commission agent, or any other agent of an independent status, provided that such persons are acting in the ordinary course of their business. However, where the activities of such an agent are devoted wholly or almost wholly on behalf of that enterprise, and where the conditions between the agent and the enterprise differ from those which would be made between independent persons, such agent shall not be considered an agent of independent status within the meaning of this paragraph. In such case the provisions of paragraph 5 shall apply.

7.   The fact that a company which is a resident of a Contracting State controls or is controlled by a company which is a resident of the other Contracting State, or which carries on business in that other State (whether through a permanent establishment or otherwise), shall not of itself constitute either company a permanent establishment of the other.

ARTICLE 6

Income From Immovable (Real) Property

1.   Income derived by a resident of a Contracting State from immovable (real) property (including income from agriculture or forestry) situated in the other Contracting State may be taxed in that other State.

2.   The term "immovable (real) property" shall have the meaning which it has under the law of the Contracting State in which the property in question is situated. The term shall in any case include property accessory to immovable (real) property, livestock and equipment used in agriculture and forestry, rights to which the provisions of general law respecting landed property apply, any option or similar right to acquire immovable (real) property, usufruct of immovable (real) property and rights to variable or fixed payments relating to the production from, or the right to work, mineral deposits, sources and other natural resources; ships, boats and aircraft shall not be regarded as immovable (real) property.

3.   The provisions of paragraph 1 shall apply to income derived from the direct use, letting, or use in any other form of immovable (real) property.

4.   Where the ownership of shares or other corporate rights in a company entitles the owner of such shares or corporate rights to the enjoyment of immovable (real)

property held by the company, the income from the direct use, letting, or use in any other form of such right to enjoyment may be taxed in the Contracting State in which the immovable (real) property is situated.

5.   The provisions of paragraphs 1, 3 and 4 shall also apply to the income from immovable (real) property of an enterprise and to income from immovable (real) property used for the performance of independent personal services.

6.   A resident of a Contracting State who is liable to tax in the other Contracting State on income from immovable (real) property situated in the other Contracting State may elect to compute the tax on such income on a net basis. In the case of the United States tax, an election to apply the preceding sentence shall be binding for the taxable year of the election and all subsequent taxable years unless the competent authority of the United States agrees to terminate the election.

ARTICLE 7

Business Profits

1.   The business profits of an enterprise of a Contracting State shall be taxable only in that State unless the enterprise carries on business in the other Contracting State through a permanent establishment situated therein. If the enterprise carries on business as aforesaid, the

business profits of the enterprise may be taxed in the other State but only so much of them as is attributable to that permanent establishment. However, profits derived from the sale of goods or merchandise of the same or similar kind as those sold, or from other business activities of the same or similar kind as those effected, through that permanent establishment may be considered attributable to that permanent establishment if it is established that such sales or activities were structured in a manner intended to avoid taxation in the State where the permanent establishment is situated.

2.   Subject to the provisions of paragraph 3, where an enterprise of a Contracting State carries on business in the other Contracting State through a permanent establishment situated therein, there shall in each Contracting State be attributed to that permanent establishment the business profits which it might be expected to make if it were a distinct and independent enterprise engaged in the same or similar activities under the same or similar conditions.

3.   In determining the business profits of a permanent establishment, there shall be allowed as deductions expenses that are incurred for the purposes of the permanent establishment, including a reasonable allocation of research and development expenses, interest, and other similar expenses and executive and general administrative expenses,

whether incurred in the State in which the permanent establishment is situated or elsewhere. A Contracting State may, consistent with its law, impose limitations on deductions, so long as these limitations are consistent with the concept of net income.

4.   Nothing in this Article shall affect the application of any law of a Contracting State relating to the determination of the tax liability of a person in cases where the information available to the competent authority of that State is inadequate to determine the profits to be attributable to a permanent establishment, provided that, on the basis of the available information, the determination of the profits of the permanent establishment is consistent with the principles stated in this Article.

5.   No business profits shall be attributed to a permanent establishment by reason of the mere purchase by that permanent establishment of goods or merchandise for the enterprise.

6.   For the purposes of the Convention, the business profits to be attributed to the permanent establishment

shall be determined by the same method year by year unless there is good and sufficient reason to the contrary.

7. For the purposes of the Convention, the term "business profits" means profits derived from any trade or business. It includes, for example, profits from manufacturing, mercantile, fishing, transportation, communications or extractive activities, and from the furnishing of personal services of another person, including the furnishing by a company of the personal services of its employees. It does not include income received by an individual for his performance of personal services either as an employee or in an independent capacity.

8. Where business profits include items of income which are dealt with separately in other Articles of the Convention, then the provisions of those Articles shall not be affected by the provisions of this Article.

9. In applying paragraphs 1 and 2 of this Article, paragraph 5 of Article 10 (Dividends), paragraph 5 of Article 11 (Interest), paragraph 4 of Article 12 (Royalties), paragraph 3 of Article 13 (Capital Gains), Article 14 (Independent Personal Services) and paragraph 2 of Article 21 (Other Income), income or gain may be attributable to a permanent establishment or fixed base even

if the income or gain is deferred until after such permanent establishment or fixed base has ceased to exist.

ARTICLE 8

Shipping and Air Transport

1.   Profits of an enterprise of a Contracting State from the operation of ships or aircraft in international traffic shall be taxable only in that State.

2.   For the purposes of this Article, the term "profits from the operation of ships or aircraft in international traffic" includes profits derived from the rental of ships or aircraft on a full (time or voyage) basis. It also includes profits from the rental of ships or aircraft on a bareboat basis by an enterprise engaged in the operation of ships or aircraft in international traffic, if such rental activities are incidental to the activities described in paragraph 1. Profits derived by an enterprise from the inland transport of property or passengers within either Contracting State are treated as profits from the operation of ships or aircraft in international traffic if

such transport is undertaken as part of international traffic by the enterprise.

3.   Profits of an enterprise of a Contracting State engaged in the operation of ships or aircraft in international traffic from the use, maintenance, or rental of containers (including trailers, barges, and related equipment for the transport of containers) used in international traffic shall be taxable only in that State.

4.   The provisions of paragraphs 1 and 3 shall also apply to profits from the participation in a pool, a joint business, or an international operating agency.

ARTICLE 9

Associated Enterprises

1.   Where:

a) an enterprise of a Contracting State participates directly or indirectly in the management, control or capital of an enterprise of the other Contracting State, or

b) the same persons participate directly or indirectly in the management, control, or capital of an enterprise of a Contracting State and an enterprise of the other Contracting State,

and in either case conditions are made or imposed between

the two enterprises in their commercial or financial relations which differ from those which would be made between independent enterprises, then any profits which would, but for those conditions, have accrued to one of the enterprises, but, by reason of those conditions, have not so accrued, may be included in the profits of that enterprise and taxed accordingly.

2.   Where a Contracting State includes in the profits of an enterprise of that State, and taxes accordingly, profits on which an enterprise of the other Contracting State has been charged to tax in that other State, and the profits so included are profits which would have accrued to the enterprise of the first-mentioned State if the conditions made between the two enterprises had been those which would have been made between independent enterprises, then that other State shall make an appropriate adjustment to the amount of the tax charged therein on those profits. In determining such adjustment, due regard shall be had to the other provisions of this Convention and the competent authorities of the Contracting States shall if necessary consult each other.

3.   The provisions of paragraph 1 shall not limit any provisions of the law of either Contracting State which permit the distribution, apportionment, or allocation of income, deductions, credits, or allowances between persons, whether or not residents of a Contracting State, owned or controlled directly or indirectly by the same interests when necessary in order to prevent evasion of taxes or clearly to reflect the income of any such persons.

ARTICLE 10

Dividends

1.   Dividends paid by a resident of a Contracting State and beneficially owned by a resident of the other Contracting State may be taxed in that other State.

2.   However, such dividends may also be taxed in the Contracting State of which the payor is a resident and according to the laws of that State, but if the beneficial owner of the dividends is a resident of the other Contracting State, the tax so charged shall not exceed:

     a) 5 percent of the gross amount of the dividends
     if the beneficial owner is a company which holds
     directly at least 10 percent of the voting shares of
     the company paying the dividends;

b) 15 percent of the gross amount of the dividends
in all other cases.

Subparagraph a) shall not apply in the case of dividends
paid by a United States person that is a Regulated
Investment Company or a Real Estate Investment Trust.
Subparagraph b) shall apply in the case of dividends paid by
a Regulated Investment Company. In the case of dividends
paid by a United States person that is a Real Estate
Investment Trust, subparagraph b) shall apply only if the
dividend is beneficially owned by an individual holding a
less than 10 percent interest in the Real Estate Investment
Trust; otherwise, the rate of withholding applicable under
domestic law shall apply.

This paragraph shall not affect the taxation of the company
in respect of the profits out of which the dividends are
paid.

3.   The term "dividends" as used in this Article means
income from shares or other rights, not being debt-claims,
participating in profits, as well as income from other
corporate rights which is subjected to the same taxation
treatment as income from shares by the laws of the State of
which the company making the distribution is a resident. The
term "dividends" also includes income from arrangements,
including debt obligations, carrying the right to
participate in profits, to the extent so characterized under

the law of the Contracting State in which the income arises.

4.   The provisions of paragraph 2 shall not apply if the beneficial owner of the dividends, being a resident of a Contracting State, carries on business in the other Contracting State of which the payor is a resident, through a permanent establishment situated therein, or performs in that other State independent personal services from a fixed base situated therein, and the dividends are attributable to such permanent establishment or fixed base. In such case the provisions of Article 7 (Business Profits) or Article 14 (Independent Personal Services), as the case may be, shall apply.

5.   A company that is a resident of one of the Contracting States and that has a permanent establishment that is subject to tax on its business profits in the other Contracting State or that is subject to tax in the other State on a net basis on its income that may be taxed in the other State under Article 6 (Income from Immovable (Real) Property) or under paragraph 1 of Article 13 (Capital Gains) may be subject in that other State to a tax in addition to the tax on profits. Such tax, however, may not exceed 5 percent of the portion of the profits of the company subject

to tax in the other State that represents the dividend equivalent amount of such profits.

6. Where a resident of a Contracting State derives profits or income from the other Contracting State, that other State may not impose any tax on the dividends paid by that resident, except insofar as such dividends are paid to a resident of that other State or insofar as the holding in respect of which the dividends are paid forms part of the business property of a permanent establishment or a fixed base situated in that other State, even if the dividends paid consist wholly or partly of profits or income arising in such other State.

ARTICLE 11

Interest

1. Interest arising in a Contracting State and beneficially owned by a resident of the other Contracting State may be taxed in that other State.

2. However, such interest may also be taxed in the Contracting State in which it arises and according to the laws of that State, but if the beneficial owner of the interest is a resident of the other Contracting State, the tax so charged shall not exceed 10 percent of the gross amount of the interest.

3. Notwithstanding the provisions of paragraph 2:

a) Interest arising in a Contracting State, derived and beneficially owned by the Government of the other Contracting State, including political subdivisions and local authorities thereof, the Central Bank or any financial institution wholly owned by that Government, or interest derived on loans guaranteed or insured by that Government, subdivision, authority or institution shall be exempt from tax in the first-mentioned State;

b) interest arising in a Contracting State shall be exempt from tax in that State if the beneficial owner of the interest is an enterprise of the other Contracting State, and the interest is paid with respect to an indebtedness arising as a consequence of the sale on credit by an enterprise of that other State, of any merchandise, or industrial, commercial or scientific equipment to an enterprise of the first-mentioned State, except where the sale or indebtedness is between related persons;

c) the United States may tax an excess inclusion with respect to a residual interest in a Real Estate Mortgage Investment Conduit in accordance with its domestic law; and

d) interest paid by a resident of a Contracting State and that is determined with reference to receipts, sales, income, profits or other cash flow of the debtor or a related person, to any change in the value of any property of the debtor or a related person or to any dividend, partnership distribution or similar payment made by the debtor to a related person also may be taxed in that State, and according to its laws, but if the beneficial owner is a resident of the other Contracting State, the gross amount of the interest may be taxed at a rate not exceeding the rate prescribed in subparagraph b) of paragraph 2 of Article 10 (Dividends).

4.   The term "interest" as used in this Convention means income from debt-claims of every kind, whether or not secured by mortgage and, subject to paragraph 4 of Article 10 (Dividends), whether or not carrying a right to participate in the debtor's profits, and in particular, income from government securities and income from bonds or debentures, including premiums or prizes attaching to such securities, bonds or debentures, as well as all other income that is treated as interest by the taxation law of the Contracting State in which the income arises. Penalty

charges for late payment shall not be regarded as interest for the purpose of this Article.

5.   The provisions of paragraphs 2 and 3 shall not apply if the beneficial owner of the interest, being a resident of a Contracting State, carries on business in the other Contracting State in which the interest arises, through a permanent establishment situated therein, or performs in that other State independent personal services from a fixed base situated therein, and the interest is attributable to such permanent establishment or fixed base. In such case the provisions of Article 7 (Business Profits) or Article 14 (Independent Personal Services), as the case may be, shall apply.

6.   Interest shall be deemed to arise in a Contracting State when the payor is a resident of that State. Where, however, the person paying the interest, whether he is a resident of a Contracting State or not, has in a Contracting State a permanent establishment or a fixed base in connection with which the indebtedness on which the interest is paid was incurred, and such interest is borne by such permanent establishment or fixed base, then such interest shall be deemed to arise in the State in which the permanent establishment or fixed base is situated.

7.   Where, by reason of a special relationship between

the payor and the beneficial owner or between both of them and some other person, the amount of the interest, having regard to the debt-claim for which it is paid, exceeds the amount which would have been agreed upon by the payor and the beneficial owner in the absence of such relationship, the provisions of this Article shall apply only to the last-mentioned amount. In such case, the excess part of the payments shall remain taxable according to the laws of each Contracting State, due regard being had to the other provisions of the Convention.

8. A resident of a Contracting State may be subject to tax in the other Contracting State in respect of interest expenses allocable to its profits attributable to a permanent establishment in the other Contracting State or subject to tax in the other Contracting State under Article 6 (Income from Immovable (Real) Property) or paragraph 1 of Article 13 (Capital Gains) over the interest paid by or from that permanent establishment or trade or business. In this case, the allocable interest expense in excess of interest paid shall be deemed to be interest arising in the other Contracting State and be beneficially owned by a resident of the first-mentioned Contracting State.

ARTICLE 12
Royalties

1.   Royalties arising in a Contracting State and beneficially owned by a resident of the other Contracting State may be taxed in that other State.

2.   However, such royalties may also be taxed in the Contracting State in which they arise and according to the laws of that State, but if the beneficial owner of the royalties is a resident of the other Contracting State, the tax so charged shall not exceed:

a) 5 percent of the gross amount of the royalties paid for the use of industrial, commercial or scientific equipment;

b) 10 percent of the gross amount of the royalties in all other cases.

3.   The term "royalties" as used in this Convention means payments of any kind received as a consideration for the use of, or the right to use, any copyright of literary, artistic or scientific work, including computer software, cinematographic films and films or tapes and other means of image or sound reproduction for radio or television broadcasting, any patent, trademark, design or model, plan, secret formula or process, or other like right or property, or for the use of, or the right to use, industrial, commercial or scientific equipment, or for information concerning industrial, commercial or scientific experience. The term "royalties" also includes payments derived from the

disposition of any such right or property which are contingent on the productivity, use or further disposition thereof.

4.   The provisions of paragraphs 1 and 2 shall not apply if the beneficial owner of the royalties, being a resident of a Contracting State, carries on business in the other Contracting State in which the royalties arise, through a permanent establishment situated therein, or performs in that other State independent personal services from a fixed base situated therein, and the royalties are attributable to such permanent establishment or fixed base. In such case the provisions of Article 7 (Business Profits) or Article 14 (Independent Personal Services), as the case may be, shall apply.

5.   Where, by reason of a special relationship between the payor and the beneficial owner or between both of them and some other person, the amount of the royalties, having regard to the use, right, or information for which they are paid, exceeds the amount which would have been agreed upon by the payor and the beneficial owner in the absence of such relationship, the provisions of this Article shall apply only to the last-mentioned amount. In such case, the excess part of the payments shall remain taxable according to the laws of each Contracting State, due regard being had to the other provisions of the Convention.

6. For purposes of this Article:

a) Royalties shall be treated as arising in a Contracting State when the payer is a resident of that State. Where, however, the person paying the royalties, whether he is a resident of a Contracting States or not, has in a Contracting State a permanent establishment or a fixed base in connection with which the liability to pay the royalties was incurred, and such royalties are borne by such permanent establishment or fixed base, then such royalties shall be deemed to arise in the State in which the permanent establishment or fixed base is situated.

b) Where subparagraph a) does not operate to treat royalties as arising in a Contracting State, and the royalties are for the use of, or the right to use, in a Contracting State any property or right described in paragraph 3, then such royalties shall be deemed to arise in that State and not in the State of which the payor is resident.

c) Notwithstanding the preceding provisions of this paragraph, payments received as consideration for the use of containers, (including trailers, barges, and related equipment for the transport of containers) used in transportation of passengers or property (other than transportation solely between places in a Contracting State), not dealt with in Article 8 (Shipping and Air Transport) shall be deemed to arise in neither Contracting State.

ARTICLE 13

Capital Gains

1. Gains or income derived by a resident of a Contracting State from the alienation of immovable (real) property situated in the other Contracting State may be taxed in that other State.

2. For the purposes of this Article, the term "immovable (real) property situated in the other Contracting State" includes immovable (real) property referred to in Article 6 (Income From Immovable (Real) Property) which is situated in that other State. It also includes shares of stock of a company the property of which consists at least 50 percent of immovable (real) property situated in that other State, and an interest in a partnership, trust or estate to the extent that its assets consist of immovable

(real) property situated in that other State. In the United States the term includes a "United States real property interest."

3. Gains from the alienation of movable property forming part of the business property of a permanent establishment which an enterprise of a Contracting State has in the other Contracting State, or of movable property pertaining to a fixed base which is available to a resident of a Contracting State in the other Contracting State for the purpose of performing independent personal services, including such gains from the alienation of such a permanent establishment (alone or with the whole enterprise) or fixed base, may be taxed in that other State.

4. Gains derived by an enterprise of a Contracting State operating ships or aircraft in international traffic from the alienation of ships, aircraft or containers operated or used in international traffic or movable property pertaining to the operation or use of such ships, aircraft or containers shall be taxable only in that State.

5. Payments described in paragraph 3 of Article 12 (Royalties) shall be taxable only in accordance with the provisions of Article 12.

6. Gains from the alienation of any property other than property referred to in paragraphs 1 through 5 shall be taxable only in the Contracting State of which the alienator is a resident.

ARTICLE 14

Independent Personal Services

1. Income derived by an individual who is a resident of a Contracting State in respect of professional services or other activities of an independent character shall be taxable only in that State unless such services are performed in the other Contracting State and he has a fixed base regularly available to him in the other Contracting State for the purpose of performing his activities. In such case, the income may be taxed in the other State, but only so much of it as is attributable to that fixed base. For this purpose, where an individual who is a resident of a Contracting State stays in the other Contracting State for a period or periods exceeding in the aggregate 183 days in any twelve-month period commencing or ending in the taxable year concerned, he shall be deemed to have a fixed base regularly available to him in that other State and the income that is derived from his activities referred to in the first

sentence of this paragraph shall be attributable to that fixed base.

2.   For the purposes of paragraph 1, the income that is taxable in the other Contracting State shall be determined in the same way as income of a resident of that other State derived in respect of professional services or other activities of an independent character. However, nothing in this paragraph shall be construed as obliging a Contracting State to grant to residents of the other Contracting State any personal allowances, reliefs and reductions for taxation purposes on account of civil status or family responsibilities that it grants to its own residents.

3.   The term "professional services" includes especially independent scientific, literary, artistic, educational or teaching activities as well as the independent activities of physicians, lawyers, engineers, architects, dentists and accountants.

ARTICLE 15

Dependent Personal Services

1.   Subject to the provisions of Articles 16 (Directors' Fees), 18 (Pensions, Social Security, Annuities, Alimony, and Child Support), 19 (Government Service) and 20 (Students, Trainees and Researchers), salaries, wages and

other remuneration derived by a resident of a Contracting State in respect of an employment shall be taxable only in that State unless the employment is exercised in the other Contracting State. If the employment is so exercised, such remuneration as is derived therefrom may be taxed in that other State.

2. Notwithstanding the provisions of paragraph 1, remuneration derived by a resident of a Contracting State in respect of an employment exercised in the other Contracting State shall be taxable only in the first-mentioned State if:

a) the recipient is present in the other State for a period or periods not exceeding in the aggregate 183 days in any twelve-month period commencing or ending in the taxable year concerned, and

b) the remuneration is paid by, or on behalf of, an employer who is not a resident of the other State, and

c) the remuneration is not borne by a permanent establishment or a fixed base which the employer has in the other State.

3. Notwithstanding the preceding provisions of this Article, remuneration in respect of an employment as a member of the regular complement of a ship or aircraft operated by an enterprise of a Contracting State in international traffic may be taxed in that Contracting

State.

ARTICLE 16

Directors' Fees

Directors' fees and other compensation derived by a resident of a Contracting State in his capacity as a member of the board of directors or any similar organ of a company that is a resident of the other Contracting State may be taxed in that other State.

ARTICLE 17

Artistes and Sportsmen

1.   Notwithstanding the provisions of Articles 14 (Independent Personal Services) and 15 (Dependent Personal Services), income derived by a resident of a Contracting State as an entertainer, such as a theater, motion picture, radio or television artiste, or a musician, or as a sportsman, from his personal activities as such exercised in the other Contracting State, may be taxed in that other State, except where the amount of the gross receipts derived by such entertainer or sportsman, including expenses reimbursed to him or borne on his behalf, from such activities does not exceed twenty thousand United States dollars ($20,000) or its equivalent in Estonian kroons for the taxable year concerned.

2.   Where income in respect of activities exercised by an entertainer or a sportsman in his capacity as such accrues not to the entertainer or sportsman but to another person, that income of that other person may, notwithstanding the provisions of Articles 7 (Business Profits), 14 (Independent Personal Services) and 15 (Dependent Personal Services), be taxed in the Contracting State in which the activities of the entertainer or sportsman are exercised, unless it is established that neither the entertainer or sportsman nor persons related thereto participate directly or indirectly in the profits of that other person in any manner, including the receipt of deferred remuneration, bonuses, fees, dividends, partnership distributions, or other distributions.

3.   The provisions of paragraphs 1 and 2 shall not apply to income derived from activities exercised in a Contracting State by a resident of the other Contracting State as an entertainer or sportsman if the visit to the first-mentioned State is wholly or mainly supported by public funds of the other State or a political subdivision or local authority thereof. In such a case, the income shall be taxable only in the Contracting State of which the entertainer or sportsman is a resident.

ARTICLE 18

Pensions, Social Security, Annuities,

Alimony, and Child Support

1.   Subject to the provisions of Article 19
(Government Service), pensions and other similar
remuneration derived and beneficially owned by a resident of
a Contracting State in consideration of past employment,
whether paid periodically or as a single sum, shall be
taxable only in that State, but the amount of any such
pension or remuneration that would be excluded from taxable
income in the other Contracting State if the recipient were
a resident thereof shall be exempt from taxation in the
first-mentioned State.

2.   Notwithstanding the provisions of paragraph 1,
payments made by a Contracting State under the provisions of
the social security or similar legislation of that State to
a resident of the other Contracting State or to a citizen of
the United States shall be taxable only in the first-
mentioned State.

3.   Annuities derived and beneficially owned by a
resident of a Contracting State shall be taxable only in
that State. The term "annuities" as used in this paragraph
means a stated sum (other than a pension) paid periodically
at stated times during a specified number of years, under an
obligation to make the payments in return for adequate and
full consideration (other than services rendered).

4. Alimony paid by a resident of a Contracting State, and deductible therein, to a resident of the other Contracting State shall be taxable only in that other State. The term "alimony" as used in this paragraph means periodic payments made pursuant to a written separation agreement or a decree of divorce, separate maintenance, or compulsory support, which payments are taxable to the recipient under the laws of the State of which he is a resident.

5. Periodic payments, not dealt with in paragraph 4, for the support of a minor child made pursuant to a written separation agreement or a decree of divorce, separate maintenance, or compulsory support, paid by a resident of a Contracting State to a resident of the other Contracting State, shall not be taxable in that other State.

ARTICLE 19

Government Service

1. Notwithstanding the provisions of Articles 15 (Dependent Personal Services) and 17 (Artistes and Sportsmen):

a) remuneration, other than a pension, paid by, or out of the public funds of a Contracting State or a political subdivision or a local authority thereof to an individual in respect of dependent personal services rendered to that State or subdivision or authority in the discharge of functions of a governmental nature shall, subject to the provisions of subparagraph b), be taxable only in that State;

b) such remuneration, however, shall be taxable only in the other Contracting State if the services are rendered in that State and the individual is a resident of that State who:

(i) is a national of that State; or

(ii) did not become a resident of that State solely for the purpose of rendering the services.

2. Subject to the provisions of paragraph 2 of Article 18 (Pensions, Social Security, Annuities, Alimony, and Child Support):

a) any pension paid by, or out of the public funds of a Contracting State or a political subdivision or a local authority thereof to an individual in respect of services rendered to that State or subdivision or authority in the discharge of functions of a governmental nature, shall, subject to the provisions of subparagraph b), be taxable only in that State;

b) such pension, however, shall be taxable only in the other Contracting State if the individual is a resident of, and a national of, that State.

ARTICLE 20

Students, Trainees and Researchers

1. a) An individual who is a resident of a Contracting State at the beginning of his visit to the other Contracting State and who is temporarily present in that other Contracting State for the primary purpose of:

(i) studying at a university or other accredited educational institution in that other Contracting State; or

(ii) securing training required to qualify him to practice a profession or professional speciality; or

(iii) studying or doing research as a

recipient of a grant, allowance, or award from a governmental, religious, charitable, scientific, literary, or educational organization;

shall be exempt from tax by that other Contracting State with respect to the amounts described in subparagraph b) of this paragraph for a period not exceeding five years from the date of his arrival in that other Contracting State.

b) The amounts referred to in subparagraph a) of this paragraph are:

(i) payments from abroad, other than compensation for personal services, for the purpose of his maintenance, education, study, research, or training;

(ii) the grant, allowance, or award; and

(iii) income from personal services performed in that other Contracting State in an aggregate amount not in excess of five thousand United States dollars ($5,000) or its equivalent in Estonian kroons for any taxable year.

2. An individual who is a resident of a Contracting State at the beginning of his visit to the other Contracting State and who is temporarily present in that other Contracting State as an employee of, or under contract with, a resident of the first-mentioned Contracting State, for the primary purpose of:

a) acquiring technical, professional, or business experience from a person other than that resident of the first-mentioned Contracting State, or

b) studying at a university or other accredited educational institution in that other Contracting State,

shall be exempt from tax by that other Contracting State for a period of 12 consecutive months with respect to his income from personal services in an aggregate amount not in excess of eight thousand United States dollars ($8,000) or its equivalent in Estonian kroons.

3. An individual who is a resident of one of the Contracting States at the time he becomes temporarily present in the other Contracting State and who is temporarily present in the other Contracting State for a period not exceeding one year, as a participant in a program sponsored by the Government of that other Contracting State, for the primary purpose of training, research, or study, shall be exempt from tax by that other Contracting State with respect to his income from personal services in respect of such training, research, or study performed in that other Contracting State in an aggregate amount not in excess of ten thousand United States dollars ($10,000) or its equivalent in Estonian kroons.

4. This Article shall not apply to income from

research if such research is undertaken not in the public interest but primarily for the private benefit of a specific person or persons.

ARTICLE 21

Other Income

1.   Items of income beneficially owned by a resident of a Contracting State, wherever arising, not dealt with in the foregoing Articles of this Convention shall be taxable only in that State.

2.   The provisions of paragraph 1 shall not apply to income, other than income from immovable (real) property as defined in paragraph 2 of Article 6 (Income from Immovable (Real) Property), if the beneficial owner of the income, being a resident of a Contracting State, carries on business in the other Contracting State through a permanent establishment situated therein, or performs in that other State independent personal services from a fixed base situated therein, and the income is attributable to such permanent establishment or fixed base. In such case the provisions of Article 7 (Business Profits) or Article 14 (Independent Personal Services), as the case may be, shall apply.

3.   Notwithstanding the provisions of paragraphs 1 and 2, items of income of a resident of a Contracting State not

dealt with in the foregoing Articles of this Convention and arising in the other Contracting State may also be taxed in that other State.

ARTICLE 22

Limitation on Benefits

1.   A resident of a Contracting State shall be entitled to all the benefits of this Convention only if it is a "qualified resident" as defined in this Article.

2.   A resident of a Contracting State is a qualified resident for a taxable year only if it is either:

a) an individual;

b) a Contracting State, a political subdivision or a local authority thereof, or an agency or instrumentality of such State, subdivision or authority;

c) a company, if:

(i) on at least half the days of the taxable year the beneficial owners of at least 50 percent of each class of the company's shares are qualified residents by reason of subparagraphs a), b), e), or f) of this paragraph, or U.S. citizens, provided that in the case of indirect ownership, each intermediate owner is a person entitled to benefits of the Convention under this paragraph;

and

(ii) amounts paid or accrued by the company during its taxable year:

A) to persons that are neither qualified residents nor U.S. citizens, and

B) that are deductible for income tax purposes in the company's State of residence (but not including arm's length payments in the ordinary course of business for services or tangible property),

do not exceed 50 percent of the gross income of the company for that year;

d) a trust or estate, if the ownership of its beneficial interests satisfies the requirement of subparagraph c)i) and its payments to persons who are not qualified residents or U.S. citizens satisfy the requirement of subparagraph c)ii);

e) a person, if:

i) beneficial interests representing at least 50 percent of the value of each class of interests in that person are substantially and regularly traded on a recognized stock exchange; or

ii) the direct or indirect owners of at least

50 percent of each class of interests in that person are persons entitled to benefits under clause i), provided that in the case of indirect ownership, each intermediate owner is a person entitled to benefits of the Convention under this paragraph;

f) a person described in subparagraph 3 b) of Article 4 (Resident) provided that more than half of the beneficiaries, members or participants, if any, in such persons are qualified residents; or

g) a United States Regulated Investment Company, or a similar entity in Estonia as may be agreed by the competent authorities of the Contracting States.

3. a) A resident of a Contracting State that is not a qualified resident shall be entitled to the benefits of this Convention with respect to an item of income derived from the other State, if:

(i) the resident is engaged in the active conduct of a trade or business in the first-mentioned State,

(ii) the income is connected with or incidental to the trade or business, and

(iii) the trade or business is substantial in relation to the activity in the other State generating the income.

b) For purposes of this paragraph, the business of making or managing investments will not be considered an active trade or business unless the activity is banking, insurance or securities activity conducted by a bank, insurance company or registered securities dealer.

c) Whether a trade or business is substantial for purposes of this paragraph will be determined based on all facts and circumstances. In any case, however, a trade or business will be deemed substantial if, for the preceding taxable year, or for the average of the three preceding taxable years, the asset value, the gross income, and the payroll expense that are related to the trade or business in the first-mentioned State equal at least 7.5 percent of the resident`s (and any related parties`) proportionate share of the asset value, gross income and payroll expense, respectively, that are related to the activity that generated the income in the other State, and the average of the three ratios exceeds 10 percent.

d) Income is derived in connection with a trade or business if the activity in the other State generating the income is a line of business that forms a part of or is complementary to the trade or business. Income is incidental to a trade or business if it facilitates the conduct of the trade or business in the other State.

4.   A resident of a Contracting State that is not a qualified resident pursuant to the provisions of paragraph 2 may, nevertheless, be granted benefits of the Convention with respect to income arising in the other Contracting State if the competent authority of that other Contracting State so determines.

5.   For the purposes of this Article, the term "recognized stock exchange" means:

a) the NASDAQ System owned by the National Association of Securities Dealers, Inc. and any stock exchange registered with the U.S. Securities and Exchange Commission as a national securities exchange under the U.S. Securities Exchange Act of 1934;

b) the Tallinn Stock Exchange (Tallinna Väärtpaberibörs); and

c) any other stock exchange agreed upon by the competent authorities of the Contracting States.

6.   The competent authorities of the Contracting States shall consult together with a view to developing a commonly agreed application of the provisions of this Article, including the publication of public guidance. The competent authorities shall, in accordance with the provisions of Article 26 (Exchange of Information and Administrative Assistance), exchange such information as is necessary for carrying out the provisions of this Article.

ARTICLE 23

Relief From Double Taxation

1.   In accordance with the provisions and subject to the limitations of the law of the United States (as it may be amended from time to time without changing the general principle hereof), the United States shall allow to a resident or citizen of the United States as a credit against the United States tax on income:

a) the Estonian tax paid by or on behalf of such resident or citizen; and

b) in the case of a United States company owning at least 10 percent of the voting stock of a company which is a resident of Estonia and from which the United States company receives dividends, the Estonian tax paid by or on behalf of the distributing company with respect to the profits out of which the dividends are paid.

2.   In Estonia, double taxation shall be avoided as follows:

a) where a resident of Estonia derives income which, in accordance with this Convention, may be taxed in the United States, unless a more favorable treatment is provided in its domestic law, Estonia shall allow as a deduction from the tax on the income of that resident, an amount equal to the income tax paid thereon in the United States (other than any such tax imposed by reason of citizenship of the United States); such deduction shall not, however, exceed that part of the income tax in Estonia, as computed before the deduction is given, which is attributable to the income which may be taxed in the United States;

b) For the purposes of subparagraph a), where a company that is a resident of Estonia receives a dividend from a company that is a resident of the United States in which it owns at least 10 percent of

its shares having full voting rights, the tax paid in
the United States shall include not only the tax paid
on the dividend, but also the appropriate portion of
the tax paid on the underlying profits of the company
out of which the dividend was paid.

3.   For the purposes of allowing relief from double
taxation pursuant to this Article, and subject to such
source rules in the domestic laws of the Contracting States
as apply for purposes of limiting the foreign tax credit,
income derived by a resident of a Contracting State which
may be taxed in the other Contracting State in accordance
with this Convention (other than solely by reason of
citizenship in accordance with paragraph 4 of Article 1
(General Scope)) shall be deemed to arise in that other
State.

ARTICLE 24

Nondiscrimination

1.   Nationals of a Contracting State shall not be
subjected in the other Contracting State to any taxation or
any requirement connected therewith, which is other or more
burdensome than the taxation and connected requirements to
which nationals of that other State in the same
circumstances, in particular with respect to residence, are
or may be subjected. This provision shall apply to persons

who are not residents of one or both of the Contracting States. However, for the purposes of United States taxation, United States nationals who are subject to tax on a worldwide basis are not in the same circumstances as nationals of Estonia who are not residents of the United States.

2.   The taxation on a permanent establishment which an enterprise of a Contracting State, or a fixed base which an individual who is a resident of a Contracting State, has in the other Contracting State shall not be less favorably levied in that other State than the taxation levied on enterprises or individuals who are residents of that other State carrying on the same activities. The provisions of this paragraph shall not be construed as obliging a Contracting State to grant to residents of the other Contracting State any personal allowances, reliefs and reductions for taxation purposes on account of civil status or family responsibilities that it grants to its own residents.

3.   Except where the provisions of paragraph 1 of Article 9 (Associated Enterprises), paragraph 7 of Article 11 (Interest), or paragraph 5 of Article 12 (Royalties) apply, interest, royalties and other disbursements paid by a resident of a Contracting State to a resident of the other Contracting State shall, for the purpose of determining the

taxable profits of the first-mentioned resident, be deductible under the same conditions as if they had been paid to a resident of the first-mentioned State. Similarly, any debts of a resident of a Contracting State to a resident of the other Contracting State shall, for the purpose of determining the taxable capital of the first-mentioned resident, be deductible under the same conditions as if they had been contracted to a resident of the first-mentioned State.

4.   Enterprises of a Contracting State, the capital of which is wholly or partly owned or controlled, directly or indirectly, by one or more residents of the other Contracting State, shall not be subjected in the first-mentioned State to any taxation or any requirement connected therewith which is other or more burdensome than the taxation and connected requirements to which other similar enterprises of the first-mentioned State are or may be subjected.

5.   Nothing in this Article shall be construed as preventing either Contracting State from imposing a tax as described in paragraph 5 of Article 10 (Dividends).

6.   The provisions of this Article shall, notwithstanding the provisions of Article 2 (Taxes Covered), apply to taxes of every kind and description imposed by a Contracting State or a political subdivision or local

authority thereof.

ARTICLE 25

Mutual Agreement Procedure

1.   Where a person considers that the actions of one or both of the Contracting States result or will result for him in taxation not in accordance with the provisions of this Convention, he may, irrespective of the remedies provided by the domestic law of those States, present his case to the competent authority of either Contracting State. The case must be presented within three years from the first notification of the action resulting in taxation not in accordance with the provisions of the Convention.

2.   The competent authority shall endeavor, if the objection appears to it to be justified and if it is not itself able to arrive at a satisfactory solution, to resolve the case by mutual agreement with the competent authority of the other Contracting State, with a view to the avoidance of taxation which is not in accordance with the Convention. Any agreement reached shall be implemented notwithstanding any time limits or other procedural limitations in the domestic law of the Contracting States.

3.   The competent authorities of the Contracting States shall endeavor to resolve by mutual agreement any difficulties or doubts arising as to the interpretation or

application of the Convention. In particular the competent
authorities of the Contracting States may agree:

a) to the same attribution of income, deductions,
credits, or allowances of an enterprise of a
Contracting State to its permanent establishment
situated in the other Contracting State;

b) to the same allocation of income, deductions,
credits, or allowances between persons;

c) to the same characterization of particular
items of income;

d) to the same characterization of persons;

e) to the same application of source rules with
respect to particular items of income;

f) to a common meaning of a term;

g) to increases in any specific dollar amounts
referred to in the Convention to reflect economic or
monetary developments;

h) to advance pricing arrangements; and

i) to the application of the provisions of domestic law regarding penalties, fines, and interest in a manner consistent with the purposes of the Convention.

They may also consult together for the elimination of double taxation in cases not provided for in the Convention.

4.   The competent authorities of the Contracting States may communicate with each other directly for the purpose of reaching an agreement in the sense of the preceding paragraphs.

ARTICLE 26

Exchange of Information and Administrative Assistance

1.   The competent authorities of the Contracting States shall exchange such information as is relevant for carrying out the provisions of this Convention or of the domestic laws of the Contracting States concerning taxes covered by the Convention insofar as the taxation thereunder is not contrary to the Convention, including the assessment of, collection of, the enforcement or prosecution in respect of or the determination of appeals in relation to the taxes covered by the Convention. The exchange of information is not restricted by Article 1 (General Scope). Any information received by a Contracting State shall be treated as secret in the same manner as information obtained under the

domestic laws of that State and shall be disclosed only to persons or authorities (including courts and administrative bodies) involved in the assessment, collection or administration of, the enforcement or prosecution in respect of, or the determination of appeals in relation to, the taxes covered by the Convention or the oversight of the above. Such persons or authorities shall use the information only for such purposes. They may disclose the information in public court proceedings or in judicial decisions.

2.   In no case shall the provisions of paragraph 1 be construed so as to impose on a Contracting State the obligation:

a) to carry out administrative measures at variance with the laws and administrative practice of that or of the other Contracting State;

b) to supply information which is not obtainable under the laws or in the normal course of the administration of that or of the other Contracting State;

c) to supply information which would disclose any trade, business, industrial, commercial or professional secret or trade process or information, the disclosure of which would be contrary to public policy (ordre public).

3.   Notwithstanding paragraph 2, laws or practices of the requested State pertaining to the disclosure of information by financial institutions, nominees or persons acting in an agency or fiduciary capacity, or respecting ownership of debt instruments or interests in a person shall not affect the authority of the requested State. The competent authorities shall have the authority to obtain and provide information notwithstanding such disclosure laws and practices. If information is requested by a Contracting State in accordance with this Article, the other Contracting State shall obtain the information to which the request relates in the same manner and to the same extent as if the tax of the first-mentioned State were the tax of that other State and were being imposed by that other State. If specifically requested by the competent authority of a Contracting State, the competent authority of the other Contracting State shall provide information under this Article in the form of depositions of witnesses and authenticated copies of unedited original documents (including books, papers, statements, records, accounts, and writings), to the same extent such depositions and documents

can be obtained under the laws and administrative practices of that other State with respect to its own taxes.

4.   Each of the Contracting States shall endeavor to collect on behalf of the other Contracting State such amounts as may be necessary to ensure that relief granted by the Convention from taxation imposed by that other State does not inure to the benefit of persons not entitled thereto.

5.   Paragraph 4 shall not impose upon either of the Contracting States the obligation to carry out administrative measures which are of a different nature from those used in the collection of its own taxes, or which would be contrary to its sovereignty, security, or public policy.

6.   For the purposes of this Article, the Convention shall apply, notwithstanding the provisions of Article 2 (Taxes Covered), to taxes of every kind imposed by a Contracting State.

7. The competent authority of the requested State shall allow representatives of the applicant State to enter the requested State to interview individuals and examine books and records with the consent of the persons contacted and the competent authority of the requested State.

ARTICLE 27

<u>Members of Diplomatic Missions and Consular Posts</u>

Nothing in this Convention shall affect the fiscal privileges of members of diplomatic missions or consular posts under the general rules of international law or under the provisions of special agreements.

ARTICLE 28

<u>Entry Into Force</u>

1.   The Governments of the Contracting States shall notify each other through diplomatic channels when the constitutional requirements for the entry into force of the Convention have been complied with.

2.   The Convention shall enter into force on the date of the later of the notifications referred to in paragraph 1, and its provisions shall have effect in both Contracting States:

a) in respect of taxes withheld at source, for amounts paid or credited on or after the first day of January of the calendar year next following the year in which the Convention enters into force;

b) in respect of other taxes on income, for taxable years beginning on or after the first day of

January of the calendar year next following the year in which the Convention enters into force.

3.   The appropriate authorities of the Contracting States shall consult within a five-year period from the date on which this Convention enters into force with respect to the application of the Convention, including the negotiations of an amendment to the Convention by mean of a protocol (if appropriate), to income derived from new technologies (such as payments received for transmission by satellite, cable, optic fibre or similar technology).

ARTICLE 29

Termination

This Convention shall remain in force until terminated by a Contracting State. Either Contracting State may terminate the Convention by giving written notice of termination, through diplomatic channels, at least 6 months before the end of any calendar year. In such event, the Convention shall cease to have effect in both Contracting States:

a) in respect of taxes withheld at source, for amounts paid or credited on or after the first day of January of the calendar year next following the year in which the notice has been given;

b) in respect of other taxes on income, for

taxable years beginning on or after the first day of January of the calendar year next following the year in which the notice has been given.

IN WITNESS WHEREOF, the undersigned, being duly authorized thereto, have signed this Convention.

DONE at Washington in duplicate, in the English and Estonian languages, both texts being equally authentic, this 15th day of January, 1998.

FOR THE UNITED STATES
OF AMERICA:

FOR THE REPUBLIC
OF ESTONIA: